OH ___!
OH MY!
Poems That Make You Laugh & Cry

Poetry by: Sondra Fry

Copyright © 2013 Sondra Fry
All rights reserved.
ISBN-10: 1481966243
EAN-13: 9781481966245

ACKNOWLEDGMENTS

I would like to thank my husband Larry, for his patients while I spent so much of my free time on this book instead with him, Thank Goodness he is a patient man!! Thank You Honey! To my brother- in- law, Al Lyons for the Illustrations, Thank You Al. A Big thank you goes out to my daughter Tabatha for reading over and over to help me correct my grammar, punctuations', & every thing else! Thank You Tabby! Thank you to my Son's TW and Todd who always had faith in me that I could do this! I can't forget the Create Space Project Team & both Andria B. & Andria C. for guiding me along the way! At Last a Huge Hug & Thank You To my two wonderful listening Grand Kids, Dylan & Layla, Thank you so much for letting me read these to you over and over until I got them right! Thank You to all my family & friends who kept telling me I could do this & I should do It, Thanks for all your encouragements Family & Friends "Thank You so much"

Love you all, Sondra Fry

TABLE OF CONTENTS

1. A prayer for Mommy 8
2. A Typical Day 9
3. Adoption 10
4. The Baby's Room 11
5. An Old Man's Broken Heart. 13
6. Camping Out 14
7. Christmas Time. 16
8. Day Dreamer 18
9. Drama Queen 19
10. Eight Seconds 20
11. Fathers Day 21
12. First Signs Of Winter 22
13. Getting The Groove 23
14. Forest Bears 25
15. Give Me The Classics 26
16. Guardian Angels 27
17. Halloween 28
18. Hillbilly Stew 29
19. In This Baptist Church I've Been 30
20. Jesus And Me By The sea 31
21. Jesus Is What It's All About 32
22. Just Sit and Relax 33
23. Kaleidoscope. 34
24. Kids Playing in the Snow 35
25. Kangaroo Jill and Izzy The Frog 36
26. Me Against the Spider 38
27. Midnight Snacks 39
28. Missing Children 40
29. My Busy Backyard 41
30. My Dog Ugly 42

TABLE OF CONTENTS

31. My Intervener 43
32. My Precious Friend 44
33. My Modern Day Knight 46
34. Night Fright 47
35. Nursery Rhymes We Shall Play 48
36. Our Small Town Fair 49
37. Radio 50
38. Romancing 51
39. Save the Pets 52
40. Secret Lovers 53
41. Snipe Hunten` 55
42. Thanksgiving Day 56
43. The Angels Were Silent 57
44. The Barn 58
45. The Battle Of Games 59
46. The Beginning of Life 60
47. The Blind Orphan 61
48. The Farmer 62
49. The Old Cowhand 63
50. The Rancher's Wife 65
51. The Storm 66
52. The Yellow Rose 67
53. The Zoo 68
54. There's a Baby in the House 69
55. Truly Love 70
56. When I Ride 71
57. Whooo Are You 72
58. Winter is Coming 73
59. Year of the Tree 74
60. A Cripple's Cry 75

A PRAYER FOR MOMMY

I was going to peek in to say goodnight,
    And then I saw my child on her knees,
Her hands were folded as she was saying her special prayer,
    One that was meant for me.

    And this is what I heard my child say:

Jesus won't you help me please,
You see my daddy has gone away,
And Mommy is very lonely,
And it was just the other day,
I saw my Mommy crying for me!
She doesn't know what to do,
And with no one else around,
I'm the only one who has to help Mommy
And keep her from feeling down.
I stood their silently and let my child finish her prayer,
Then I quietly stepped into the room,
When suddenly I felt a strange presence there.
And saw a light that I thought was a glare from the moon.
Then a sudden thought came to me,
That everything will be alright,
I just got to believe and hold on…..
    And I'm going to start tonight.

A TYPICAL DAY

First thing in the morning, I trip over the skates,
    Trying to get to the bathroom before I wait too late!
The alarm is still a buzzin`, and the coffee is a little strong,
    The husband is rushin` to work and the kids are hustlin` along.

Now I've got to get all my housework done, it's gotta be done by noon,
    For my first soap opera show will be startin` soon.
I grab my coffee and head for my favorite chair,
    Call my girlfriend on the phone to see who's with who and where.

Now the kids are out of school and supper is on it's way,
    Husband will be coming home soon, asking me what I did all day?
I will say "The usual dear, a woman's work is never done."
    And for my reward, he will softly kiss my ear,
And tenderly pinch my buns.

ADOPTION

A child is born with no place to go.
    As I'm looking in the window,
I'm wondering who is going to watch that baby grow?
    It's important right now that the baby has a mother's touch,
Oh how I would love to go pick that baby up.
    To love it, hold it, and give the baby a gentle hug,
And to say I'll give you all the above.
    A home and happiness I can give to you,
If they will only let my adoption go through.
    Oh please God of all the prayers we ever asked,
Answer this prayer like you always did in the past....

Now at last the baby has a home!
A mother and Father she can call her own.

THE BABY'S ROOM

There's a baby room full of toys
    And a rockin' chair in the corner.
A chest of drawers by the window
    Grandpa's playing his Blues harp by Hohner.

Baby's now sound a sleep
    In the cradle I use to lay.
It was kept in the barn
    In a loft of hay.

The northern star is shinning bright
    Glowing in the room.
It's the perfect natural light
    That bounces off the moon.

Silently we leave the room
    So baby wont awake.
Morning will be coming soon
    So be quiet for goodness sake!

An Old Mans Broken Heart

AN OLD MAN'S BROKEN HEART

While I was sittin' in my old rockin' chair
    I was wondering if my son really cared?
You see, I'm old and all alone.
    My son is grown, I'm without a home.

He's put me in this place you see,
    Where the old get older,
And eventually....
    You lose your memories.

When I was put in here you know,
    I was told it was the place to go.
But now I'm so lonely, I'd rather be
    Buried under some big Willow tree.

One day my son came for a visit and…
    To show his respects
They said, "you better sit down sir"
    We'll tell you what to expect….

You see, your father died the other day
    We had to bury him right away.
On the stone above his head,
    This is how the words were read…..

"Here lies an old man with a broken heart
    No one cared, so he fell apart."
Now he has a place to be
    Resting under the big willow tree.

CAMPING OUT

School's out for the summer,
We're going to have some fun alright,
Dad's taking us on a camping trip,
We're going to leave tonight.
Mom says go pack your things,
But the glamour has to stay,
So out goes my curling iron, blow dryer, even my hair spray!
Now we're in the station wagon,
To the mountains we go
We're setting up tents in the forest called Medicine Bow,
We've got our campfire going,
And smores we're going to make,
I swore I heard coyotes howling,
Mom says for goodness sake!
We're singing our campfire song,
First and last was the one called "The Bear"
It's about a bear being out in the woods a way out there,
And he sized up me, I sized up him and so on and so on
Well…that was enough for me,
So in our sleeping bags we went,
Boy I tell you I made sure we zipped up our tent.
Just as I was falling asleep, wouldn't you know it, I came up off my feet
in a flying heap and I did this two yard leap…..
All because of a bear, who decided to give us a scare,

CAMPING OUT

He made some noise in the picnic area,
Which caused all this hysteria!
Everyone in the camp ran like we had Malaria!!
Needless to say…..
Camping again for us is far away
Dad says our next outing will be
Disneyland or just a good home movie!

CHRISTMAS TIME

I love the feeling of Christmas,
    The ground covered with snow,
Everyone is hustling around,
    Wondering which store they should go.

The lights are blinking ever so pretty,
    On our Christmas tree,
With gifts all around it,
    Making everyone wonder joyfully.

Eggnog seems really special,
    Especially this time of year,
With all the other goodies,
    And we will do caroling with a cheer.

Haystack riding can be really fun,
    And oh those Christmas programs,
Makes you feel like your number one!

    But the most special moment has to be…
When you peek to see Santa on Christmas Eve!
    With unbelieving eyes,
And a heart full of joy,
    We go back to our beds,
Remembering our list of toys.

CHRISTMAS TIME

Finally Christmas day is here,
    And with our P.J's on,
We rush to the Christmas tree,
    To see what Santa's brung.

And what a joyous day Christmas is each year,
I'd like to say to all of you…
Merry Christmas and good cheer!

DAY DREAMER

As I was walking down town one day,
I stopped to do some window shopping on my way.
And there it was…The most beautiful dress I've ever seen!
With matching shoes fit for a queen.

They had satin ribbon for my hair,
Fine silk stockings I shall wear.
Like Cinderella at the ball,
I'll feel like the fairest of them all.

And when the clock strikes at midnight,
Surely you'll see,
I will be back at the window dreamin' Joyfully!

DRAMA QUEEN

I fell down and hurt my knee,
Then went screaming to Mama
And all she said to me;
Oh don't be a drama queen!

I went to school the very next day,
And the teacher asked what happened to me?
I said it was horrible!
And required some emergency,
Then the teacher said to me…Oh don't be a drama queen!

So I went about my day,
And after school the teacher said I had to stay,
For I have to practice for our Drama Play,
The teacher came to me,
And said I have this perfect part you can be,
You will be the drama queen,
I said oh no!! not me!!
For my mama says to me:
Don't be a drama queen!

EIGHT SECONDS

The next bull up in the chute,
    Is a bull named Bodacious!
The bull rider takes off his hat, say's a prayer,
    The crowd Gasps…This will be like riding a cactaceous!
He mounts on the eighteen hundred pounds of pure hate,
    And for eight seconds it will be the longest ride of his life!
Then it happens…..They open the gate,
    With only two seconds to go,
The Announcer announces "cowboy down"!
    Now it's time for the bullfighter to distract the bull,
So with his speed, agility, and his ability to anticipate the bulls next move,
    The bull riders life is now in his hands!
The crowd roars…and they all stand,
    With looks of desperation…
They watch as the bullfighter maneuvers and dances around the bull,
    And the crowd thrives on the thrill,
While the bullfighter tries not to get killed!
    The bullfighter exiled the bull from the arena,
The crowd goes wild!!
    Another bull goes into the chute,
Another eight seconds to be counted down,
    Are you ready?
Eight, seven, six, five, four, three, two, one
    He won, He won!!!

FATHER'S DAY

I have a friend who is very special to me
    He's very understanding
And supportive he will always be
    He's always there when I need him
And listens to all my troubles
    I whish I could do more for him
Or maybe give him a double.
    But since there's not two of me,
One is all you get,
    But I love you more then two,
And Dad this is what I'm trying to say:
    Have a very Happy Father's day!

FIRST SIGNS OF WINTER

There's a chill in the air,
And a spider in the corner of the room.
The bugs are coming in,
I think winter will be here soon.

The animals are movin` their babies,
For shelter they are tryin` to find.
Grandpa says it's maybe,
The first winter sign.

Cow's are movin` closer together,
For they even know,
It won't be much longer,
Until we have our first winter snow.

The trees are turning colors,
Fall is coming early this year,
It's getting time to dig out
Our fall and winter gear!

We're cutting wood for fires
To warm our hands and feet.
Puttin` chains on our tires,
And stuffin` blankets behind our pickup seats.

Everything is almost ready,
For the winter that's on its way,
It won't be much longer,
Until we see that first winter day!

GETTING THE GROOVE

Hold your head up,
    Now make your feet move,
Start dancing…..
    Don't worry about someone watching,
Just feel the music…
    Now start prancing…
Back this way, now that way…
    Feeling the groove? Oh Ya!!
You've got the move…
    Put your arms up,
Now put your arms down,
    Then turn your self round and round…
Oh Ya!! You've got the groove.
    Ok now its time to do some boot scootin boogie.
Turn your radio on…
    Feel the music….
Do the dance…
    Don't you just feel the romance?
Oh Ya!! You've got the groove!!

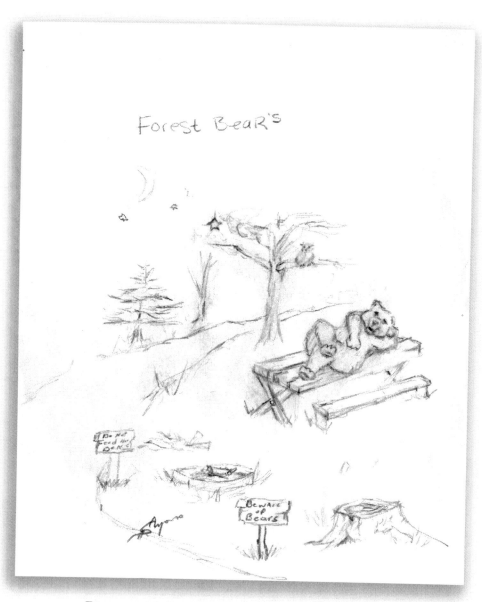

Picture with bear laying on the picknic table

FOREST BEARS

I wish I was a forest bear,
    Sleeping at night in the evening air,
Under the stars listening to the sounds of the night,
    Waiting for the morning light.

Running wild in the forest trees,
    Trying to find those fresh berries,
Headin` for the river banks,
    To catch some fish, and tear up planks,
Now down the road I go….
    Looking for the picnic area,
To scare some people for their food,
    I will surely cause some hysteria,
I will get to eat…eating at last,
    But I must hurry…
For those forest rangers are getting fast!
    They don't appreciate us hungry bears,
They prefer we stay w-a-y out there!!

GIVE ME THE CLASSICS

What ever happened to the classic TV shows?
　If I said a horse is a horse of course have you ever heard of a talking horse?
Of course the show is Mr. Ed,
　And who had the ability to fly with a passing breeze?
Of course sister Bertrille in the flying Nun!
　And what was Gomer Pyle's favorite saying? gaw---leee,
Quinton McHale on McHale's navy always saying "Great jumping Jehoshaphat"!
　And Gilligan's Island with the skipper always yelling " hey little buddy where you at"?
Those were the times you could sit and watch a show,
　With no worries and what was said, and rated for the young and old,
I just loved Happy Days with The Fonzi, Richie, Joanie, and Potsie,
　And how about Hogan's Hero's, now you no they weren't really Nazis'!
Remember Dennis the Menace? Poor Dennis always getting into trouble,
　And Mr. Wilson got enough knocks that I'm sure he saw doubles!
Green Acres was the place to be…
　That's if you wanted to be a farmer and had a wife willing to leave the city!
And you might just find some junk that you could use on that farm,
　Just go to Sanford and Son salvage yard,
Yep give me these old classic TV shows
　I still say they are the best you'll ever know!

GUARDIAN ANGELS

Have you ever seen an Angel
    Lying in your bed at night?
That has a halo that glows,
    With radiant rays of light.
She's always wearing a white lace gown
    made of Material that's unknown.
And you lay and wonder…..am I still at home?

    You're thinking in your mind,
Can this be heaven or is this a sign?
    Yet you are at peace, and everything is fine.
    The Angels they just come to see,
Making sure everyone is resting peacefully!

HALLOWEEN

Halloween… oh what a fright!
    Those spooky little children,
My what a sight!
    Pumpkins glowing all down the road,
Witches and goblins and croaky toads.
    So many frightful creatures,
Made from someone's imagination.
    I wonder what will be their next creation?
The most fun part of Halloween….
    Is going trick - or- treating,
All those goodies you get,
    Along with those spooky feelings!
Haunted houses and big black cats,
    Flying broom sticks and pointed witches hats.
When you hear of all these things,
    Don't you know what the night will bring?
Yes my children…It's only Halloween!

HILLBILLY STEW

A potato here, and a carrot there,
    A fly or two, no one cares,
A little meat, a little fat,
    I wonder what would happen,
If I tossed in a hair from a cat?
    Here's some salt, fresh tomatoes too,
I think I'll throw in some horse radish root,
    A little sand, for that crunchy grit,
A worm or two, and a toss of tobacco spit,
    Now if you can eat this hillbilly stew,
I'll write a cookbook just for you!

IN THIS BAPTIST CHURCH I'VE BEEN

I don't know what kind of instruments they are,
    In this Baptist church I've been,
But when you hear the music start,
    You know the spirit is within.

It's the most beautiful melody,
    So pleasant to my ear,
You could say its melodiousness,
    That you will hold so dear.

The worships are through their music,
    In this church I've found,
Down in the valley of Southern Kentucky,
    Where people come to praise from all around.

There is no words that can explain,
    What you're feelin` here,
But the music will bring you back,
    Year after year!

It's the line-out hymnody,
    That makes the music so serene,
It's the remedy for healing,
    In this Baptist church I've been!

JESUS AND ME BY THE SEA

I was going for my daily walk,
    Down by the sea,
When I notice footsteps,
    That where following me.

It really freaked me out,
    For I thought it was a sign,
A sign that it was my time to go.

When ahead I could see...
    A man who appeared to be injured,
And he needed help from me,
    Here I was all alone,
And I had to help this stranger on my own.

With strength that I never had,
    I lifted this man and carried him,
For at least a mile and a half.

I got him to where he needed to be,
    Then I said a prayer upon my knees,
Lord now I understand,
    It was you that was following me,
I should have no doubts in your plan,

For It was you...Giving me a helping hand,
    And then Jesus said to me,
"Believe in me, and I will always walk with you by the sea".

JESUS IS WHAT IT'S ALL ABOUT

I want to scream and shout,
    Jesus is what it's all about!
I want to sing and dance,
    It's Jesus I love and romance.
Without the Savior in my life,
    I could not survive,
He's in my heart to stay,
    You cannot scare him away.
It's Jesus that's turned my life around,
    And if you don't believe then you lost what I have found,
All I had to do was hold up my hands,
    Then I yelled "Welcome Jesus" welcome to my home.
Hallelujah I will never again be alone!

JUST SIT AND RELAX

He says just sit back and relax,
    Relax!! How can I relax,
When I feel like I've taken ex-lax,
    I'm on the run all the time,
I don't even have time to enjoy the sunshine,
    And he tells me to just sit and relax,
I have to go to the store,
    And get back in time to do the chores,
Then cook the kids supper,
    While he sits and lets his mouth run like water going threw a scupper,
And he tells me to just sit and relax!
    Well I'm going to have some well deserved fun,
I just booked me a cruise for one,
    Now I'll get to relax and enjoy the sun,
And when you call me on the phone,
    Because you need me to come home,
I'm going to tell you…..Just sit and relax!
    Don't worry about the million and one,
All the things that have to be done,
    I'll see you when I get back,
So just sit and relax!

KALEIDOSCOPE

As I rotate my kaleidoscope,
    The objects go tumbling around,
Creating such beautiful symmetrical patterns,
    That will for sure leave you spellbound.

Your eyes search for unusual shapes and colors,
    That you will find like no other,
And as I turn my kaleidoscope round and round,
    I am mesmerized by the designs that I have found.

I'm like a child with a new toy,
    My kaleidoscope gives me such curiosity and joy,
I have found magic inside this round device,
    Like dragons, flowers, shapes and sizes.

And to my surprise my kaleidoscope is calming,
    Great relaxation and even good for meditation,
I am glad I have my kaleidoscope to explore,
    I think everyone should have one or more!

KIDS PLAYING IN THE SNOW

Snow is falling to the ground,
    And the clouds are covering the sun,
Winter is all around,
    And building a snowman will be fun.

We will get our sleds out of the shed,
    And head for the highest hill,
When we get to the bottom,
    Our faces will be red,
And our noses will be a bit chilled.

KANGAROO JILL AND IZZY THE FROG

Kangaroo Jill and Izzy the frog,
    Best friends they were indeed,
Kangaroo Jill ate leaves and shrubs,
    And Izzy the frog ate all kinds of icky bugs.

Jill was tall and strong,
    Izzy was small and long,
They were the oddest pair to see,
    But they sure enjoyed each others company!

Kangaroo Jill could hop like she was a locomotive with speed,
    Whereas Izzy the frog her hop was short and steady,
As she was superseded by her friend kangaroo Jill,
    Who could actually hop right over a hill!

There's a surprise in store for these two friends,
    For kangaroo Jill is about to have twins,
But when Izzy heard the news,
    She bowed her head…
She thought for sure their friendship would be dead!

KANGAROO JILL AND IZZY THE FROG

As Izzy started to walk away,
    Jill hollered for Izzy to come back, come back, don't leave!
For you are my family!!!
    Izzy looked up with surprise,
You still want me in your life?

Yes!! Yes!! Kangaroo Jill said,
    Separating us will never be,
You will always be our family.

ME AGAINST THE SPIDER

When I walked into the room
I saw a spider near the door.
It was the scariest creature I've ever seen
OH Gosh, it had eight legs….or more!

My voice screeched with panic
Wondering what I should do,
I get my baseball bat, spray, and armor,
Reinforcements too!

It's the biggest spider I've ever seen
Maybe the biggest in the world!
I did my funny little dance
Then gave the bat a hurl.

I didn't make the spider happy
So he came after me,
I danced on top of the couch and chair
As snappy as I could be!

My husband came into the room
To see what the excitement was,
I pointed to the spider with fear on my face,
My husband laughed and said, "do you want me to get the Mace?"

The idea of mace sounded good to me
But my husband thought it was time to end my misery,
So with a swat of his hand, the spider I fear no more
For my knight in shinning armor squashed it on the floor!

MIDNIGHT SNACKS

Have you ever gotten up in the middle of the night?
    Just to get a little snack,
You're really quiet not to wake any one up,
    But you just didn't know your parents set a mouse trap!!
And as you're screaming and jumping up and down,
    Everyone in the house awoke and is running around,
The house is still dark inside,
    So you and the kitchen chairs collide,
Your mother thinks its intruders,
    Your siblings think you're playing games on the computer,
But your father knows you're getting a snack,
    He announces for everyone just to relax,
Well father says no more snacks in the middle of the night,
    For it creates to much of a fright,
So now I take them with me when I go to bed,
    I share my snacks with my favorite dog who's name is Fred.

MISSING CHILDREN

Missing children, where have they gone?
Are they lost or stolen?
You fear there is something wrong!
You shiver from fear, shed a tear, knowing they are not here.

We share the parents sorrow,
Pray for the child a tomorrow.
We thank God our children are at home,
But the pain is the same as if they are your own.

We're shocked and hurt when a child goes missing,
We need to give our children the strength from this happening.
Let's use programs, schools, churches and police,
There's so many options, why wait for a news release?

Let's educate our children, make them understand,
Strangers don't offer a friendly helping hand.
We must teach them programs, give them safe numbers to call,
Don't give them any reason to rely on strangers at all!

Have your child call you certain times of the day,
So you will know if they are at home or play.
Most important ….If a stranger approached your child,
What would your child do or say?

MY BUSY BACKYARD

My backyard is busy as it can be……
    I'm hearing the song of Chickadee's.
With beauty and grace the butterflies go by,
    Purple Martins in their home up high.
Yellow Throated Warblers, where have you been?
    Such a rare visit from the Wrens.
Hi there Mr. Brown Thrasher with your eyes of yellow,
    You're sure a cute little fellow!
A yellow bellied Flycatcher feathers of olive-green,
    You're the most curious bird I have ever seen.
There's a Nuthatch on a tree trunk, he's going up,
    And now he's going down!
A Turtle Dove I see, eating seeds on the ground.
    A Redheaded Woodpecker, he's looking at me,
A bright red Cardinal sitting in the Jack Pine tree.
    Humming birds are filling up
With nectar off the trumpet vines.
    Baltimore Oriole's are picking
On a watermelon rind.

Oh this Busy backyard of Mine!

MY DOG UGLY

I got this ugly dog from a shelter,
    It's the ugliest you've ever seen,
I didn't pick her, she actually picked me,
    I couldn't think of a name…So Ugly it shall have to be!
I was taking ugly for a walk one day,
    And she got out of her leash and ran away,
So I yelled down the street commanded her to come back……
    Ugly!! hey ugly!! Come over here now!
But what I didn't see before I opened my mouth,
    Was a lady bending down,
She stood up and looked right at me!
    Then she gave me a whack with a newspaper stack,
Which brought me down to me knees!
    Ugly she said, is that what you called me?
Well look at you now, down on your knees,
    Who's ugly now? For it sure isn't me!
Well…after my ordeal and my pride being hurt,
    I decided to rename ugly…..
Now I call her starburst!

MY INTERVENER

You have taught me to praise the Lord…..Amen!
    And inspired me to sing……Hallelujah!
You have showed me Angels exists,
    And lead me to the path right to yah!

My feet are dancing to your rhythm…
    Of Hallelujahs and Amens!
My heart is pounding of love and praises,
    I've found the Lord within!!

I had sorrows that flowed like the Cayenne River,
    And troubles that lead me astray,
I would help no one for I was not a giver,
    But that has changed, for you showed me the way!

The world now seems brighter,
    And the air smells alot cleaner,
My heart is so much lighter,
    And I have the Lord as my Intervener!

MY PRECIOUS FRIEND

With you it's all about voiceless communication....
Always knowing what to say,
But never having to say it.
When no one seems to be listening....
You hear.
When I hurt but don't show it,
You know.
When I turn away to hide my tears....
You see.
When I feel like I can't get through to anyone,
You understand.
You know everything there is to know about me....
What worries me.
What keeps me up at night.
What shames me so badly.
What gives me terrible fright.
Most importantly though, none of those things bother you....
You've restored my faith in people.
You've proved that there is a thing called "True Friendship."
We all need someone in our life....
To talk to.
To run to.
In times of stress or strife.
A friend who's always there....
Throughout the years
A friend we know will take away our fears.
A friend who's always near....
Waiting for our call.

MY PRECIOUS FRIEND

To wipe away our tears.
Lift us when we fall.
A loving friend indeed….
On whom we can depend.
To fulfill our every need.
Thank You! Precious friend.

MY MODERN DAY KNIGHT

Will you be my knight in shinning armor,
    And sweep me off my feet?
Will you romance me with love and honor,
    Until the sun and rainbow meet.

Will you let me be the princess
    From the fairytale land?
And you be my modern day knight
    With a world full of love in your hands.

And on our white steed
    We both shall ride,
To our fairytale castle,
    Where we will share our love and pride.

NIGHT FRIGHT

There's a shadow lingering in the night,
    The south wind is blowing,
Trees are creaking,
    It gives me a fright!
I hear noises that aren't really there!
    And feel crawly things on my body and in my hair!
With my room so dark,
    I imagine all sorts of things....
I hide under my covers....
    Scared to death what the night would bring!
Some how I always manage to close my eyes,
    Only to wake up to a beautiful blue sky,
All those scary night things will have to wait,
    Till I go to bed again, in the night, when it's very late!

NURSERY RHYMES WE SHALL PLAY

One, two, three, four, I hear a knock on my door.
    Nursery rhymes we shall play,
For mother has gone away.
    Five, six, lets pickup sticks,
Is what we'll play while mother is sick.
    Nick knack give the dog a bone,
I wonder when mother is coming home?
    Dear me! Dear my!
The cupboard is bare, I wonder why?
    Mother has so many children,
She doesn't know what to do.
    She feels like the old lady who lived in the shoe!
There was a Mary, who had a little lamb,
    Didn't you know, she named him Sam!
And how about little Boy Blue,
    Who forgot to blow his horn.
I think he was really playing in the corn.
    A Tisket a Tasket.
What ever happened to that green and yellow basket?
    Do you remember Little Miss Muffet?
If so, tell me….What is a tuffet?
    What really happened to that poor little spider?
I think she really drank him in a cup of apple cider!!!!

OUR SMALL TOWN FAIR

Carmel apples and cotton candy,
    A silly clown whose name is Brandy.
The balloons are floating in the air,
    Today we're going to our small town fair.

I am going to go high,
    On a Ferris wheel ride.
Then upside down,
    In a box that goes round and round.

I will eat hotdogs with relish and mustard,
    Popcorn that is smothered with hot melted butter.
Funnel cakes are twisted in little piles,
    Snow cones always bring on smiles!

I know this will bring,
    Belly aches tonight.
But a little Pepto-Bismol
    Will make it alright.

RADIO

I can inspire you to sing,
Maybe even dance.
Sometimes I bring on tears,
Sometimes I bring on romance.

Everyday you turn me on,
And everyday I sing you a tune.
And if you listen long enough,
I'll give you the news at noon.

And don't you know, My name is radio!
And I even have a variety of talk shows.
I offer music for the listening ear,
Weather for those who live far and near.

I don't cost much,
So go ahead and turn me on.
Call up your favorite DJ,
And they'll even play your favorite song.

ROMANCING

Put a log on the fire,
    Rumor has it that the kids won't be home tonight,
So get out your Victoria Secret attire,
    For we're going to be romancing alright.
I'm serving wine with our dinner,
    And turning the music down low.
A little slow dancing should be a winner,
    And for the evening I'll even let you call me Georgio!
I bought some sweet plumeria massage oil,
    To relax you the whole night through.
And when we wake up in the morning,
    Hello!!! It will be Deja Vu!

SAVE THE PETS

Such sad eyes looking at me,
    Not one, not two, but three!
Three little puppies in a cage,
    Waiting for a home,
Or someone to take them away!
    I reach in and scratch an ear,
Rub their head, and I shed a tear!
    Such a good friend you would make,
But only one I can take.
    The Humane Society tries there best,
To locate homes for those lost pets.
    But they need your help you see,
Rather it be donations, adoptions, or volunteering!
    So help out when you can,
Lend the animal shelters your helping hand,
    Let's all pitch in and just do what you can,
And the Animal shelters will find them a home
    One that will be their own!

SECRET LOVERS

Secretly we meet on those lonely nights,
    Just to be held and make it alright.
Tenderly we make love and slowly we sigh,
    Our soft touch of kisses,
And we whisper in the night.

Your soul enters into me and mine into you,
    We share our differences and our points of view.
And while we lay here silently,
    We wish for each other eternity,
And until we meet for the next time,
    I hope to see you in the grocery line!

Snipe Hunting

SNIPE HUNTEN`

When I first moved to the Sandhills,
The first thing I was asked,
Would you like to go snipe huntin`? ......
We'll have a real blast.
So with gunnysacks and flashlights,
To the hills we went,
I was sure it would be fun;
The way it was explained, it would be a cinch!

Now I'm waiting patiently for them birds to come to me,
Then I hear the sound of the truck….
I'm just a little bit scared, but not very much!
Now I was from a big city,
And being alone in them hills, was making me feel a bit silly,
I finally realized it was just a joke, boy did I start to choke!
It was a long hike back to town,
I didn't know which way to go, up or down,
I finally made it back to the house,
Everyone there was quiet as a mouse,
Yep… they were all there waitin` for me,
Because they all busted out laughin` and smilen` for surely you see,
A snipe huntin` sucker was made out of me!!

THANKSGIVING DAY

Thanksgiving day in our house,
    Always starts the evening before.
For Mama says baking pies,
    Can be quiet a chore!

Papa is out chopping logs,
    So we can keep our company warm.
They will be arriving soon,
    To eat with us on our farm.

Big brother is out hunting for turkey,
    For us to eat on this thankful day.
Mama always brings out the beef jerky,
    For us kids to snack, and keep us out of her way!

Mama bakes all day and half the night,
    To make our day a special one.
We have a lot to be thankful for,
    For mama always gets her chores all done.

With plenty of turkey,
    And plenty of Grub,
Our bellies are full,
    And the dishes are in the old round tub.

With the old round tub full of dishes,
    Down to the river we will go,
To give mama a break,
    We'll wash them really slow!

THE ANGELS WERE SILENT

A touch of a kiss was felt upon my face.
    I wonder who?
A hug I once embraced,
    Is a memory that can't be erased.
I watched the leaf softly hit the ground,
    There is no sound.
I smell Lilac in the air,
    Even though they cannot be found.

Everything about me seems brighter,
    And the music… It's so delightful,
Songs of earthly creatures are less frightful.

I am at home yet not alone,
    The Angels are here again…
They are silent.
    They want to be near,
To ease your pain to ease your fear.

Now do you understand?
    It's Angels with their plan,
You only have one thing left to do…
    That's hold out your hand!
The Angels are silent.

THE BARN

When I go visiting my grandparents on the farm,
    First thing I do is head for the barn.
I love to play in the raft of hay,
    Milk the cow and spray the cat,
Brush the horses and scratch their backs.
    I even have a little pet raccoon,
He likes me too feed him with a wooden spoon.
    Oh how I love to play on Grandpa's antique tractor,
I even tried to build one with my erectors!
    I fed the chickens and gathered their eggs,
Cleaned the stalls and laid down fresh hay.
    For grandpa says that's a great way to start your day!
Oh how I love to go to my grandparent's farm,
    And I always head for my favorite hangout…. the barn.

THE BATTLE OF GAMES

DSI one, two or three,
Angry birds....what the heck are these?
Xbox, Playstation, Nintendo and a device called Wii,
Whatever happened to Scrabble, Checkers, or even Monopoly?
And didn't you just love that classic game of battling robots....
Rock`em, - Sock`em, and the worst that could happen...
Is that you'd lock`em up!
Or how about your strategies' for Parcheesi!
Give me the old classic games,
Yahtzee, Chess, Backgammon or even Operation.
What are the kids learning from these electronic games of this new generation?
For me, it just puts my mind in a frame of desperation!
I'll take the board games,
You take the ones that have to be plugged in,
And when the electricity goes out...
We'll see who wins!!

THE BEGINNING OF LIFE

I feel safe, secure, and warm
    I'm in a place where I feel no harm.
Soon I will see a new world beginning
    For I am about to be born.

New faces I now see
    A warm breast, I am pleased
I hear my mother's heart beating away
    I was born upon this day.

I know my mother by her gentle touch,
    Her smell pleases me very much.
Soon I will be arriving in my new home,
    Again I will feel safe, secure, and warm.

THE BLIND ORPHAN

As I was walking past a orphan's home one day,
   I stopped there for a moment just to watch the children play.
There alone a boy was standing, so I asked him "why ?"
   He turned with eyes that could not see, then he began to cry.
When people come to adopt children and see that I am blind,
   They always take some other child, and I am left behind.
I have never felt a mother's touch,
   And never seen a daddy's smile,
But when I walk the streets of heaven,
   Where all the blind can see,
Just like the other kids,
   There will be a home for me!

THE FARMER

Down on the farm,
    Where the farmers grow,
Wheat, Corn, Sorghum all in a roll.
    They are up before sunrise,
Down after Dawn,
    But the farmers keep working
While whistling their favorite song!
    The dust is blowing everywhere,
But the farmer is still out there!
    He hears the humming of the tractor all day long,
Yet he's still whistling that favorite song!
    His eyes are tired,
And his bones are weak,
    But he knows the crop won't keep,
So he keeps working around the clock
    The farmers work…work…work…just never stops!

THE OLD COWHAND

Cowboy hats and old leather boots,
    Rusted up spurs, and a bottle of booze,
A broken down horse, a saddle worn through,
    He traded his bedroll for a home cooked goose.

Coffee is on the fire, and the beans are in the pan,
    The coyotes are howlin',
The only thing he's missin' is a woman's helping hand.

    The day is breakin' in the orange colored sky,
The cowboy needs a bathin, but he's to shy,
    So the smell of this man is surely to be,
Of an old cowhand in the rough Country!

The Ranchers Wife

THE RANCHER'S WIFE

There's dishes in the sink
    And the house is upside down.
The bedrooms are so cluttered
    You can't even get around.
Supper is a-burning
    And the telephone is ringin`,
The kids are yelling,
    And the old man is a-drinkin`.
There's curlers in my hair,
    And the doorbells a-dingin.
It's the U.P.S. man,
    With a C.O.D. he's bringin`.
The dogs got the cat,
    And the cows are out of the barn.
The chickens are a-cluckin`
    And I'm out of yarn.

Well the evening is coming nearer,
    And the washing still needs done.
And I don't need another day,
    That ends like this one!

THE STORM

You came along and turned my world upright!
Now it's tilted again,
I think I lost a friend!
What happened to the promise?
To always talk things over,
Never assume someone else is right.
You let the thunder and lighting strike!
It's ok, I'm still here
When you are ready to come out of the rain.

THE YELLOW ROSE

I give to you this yellow rose,
    Yellow reminds me of the sunshine you spread,
You have bestowed your love to me,
    The thorns I have removed…No blood you will ever shed.
The yellow rose reminds me of you,
    Like the sun that radiates heat,
You warm my heart with rhythmatic beats.
    This yellow rose has a aromatherapy scent,
Like you, wonderful, sweet, and very elite!

So my yellow rose to me,
    Will you please consent to marrying me?
Take this rose from my hand,
    As a gesture you understand,
And please agree to be my wife,
    Forever we will be; through Eternal life.

THE ZOO

Have you ever been to a children's Zoo?
    Did you feed the monkeys? Watch the kangaroos?
Oh and you should hear them big old bears,
    Boy they sure can give a kid a scare!
And those swans they are so sleek,
    You ought to see those flamingos silly beaks!
There's lions and tigers too…
    Of course you always see them in a zoo.
I think what I like most of all,
    Is those giraffes because they're so big and tall.
Elephants they're ok,
    But they don't do nothing but stand around all day!
Orangutans and big baboons,
    I like to watch them eat at noon,
There's a lot more to see when you go to the zoo,
    Certainly a lot of things kids can do!

THERE'S A BABY IN THE HOUSE

I'm picking up toys from the living room floor,
    I go in the kitchen, Oh My! There's more!
Pots and pans are everywhere,
    A cookie or two smashed in baby's hair,
A bath is due, but baby don't care.
    Baby scrambles and heads for the door,
To see what else baby can explore!
    I run to save the cat! Baby was sitting on it's lap!
    Tippy cups are upside down,
There are bottles never to be found.
    The house is full of giggles, what's and why's,
A bare bottom baby, she's not too shy.
    Baby is napping on the floor,
Shhh, be quiet, quiet as a mouse,
    There's a sleeping baby in the house.

TRULY LOVE

You are as soft as the summer breeze
    And the smell about you is a tease
Your smile is like the shinning sun
    And your hair soft like lambs wool that's just been spun

You have such a graceful way to your walk
    And I love your voice when you talk
Your soft hands have such a gentle touch
    That makes me love you very much

Your eyes sparkle with a glittery glow
    That's why I don't want to ever let you go
For all these things I say above
    Truly is Truly Love

WHEN I RIDE

When I ride my horse,
    I feel wild and free,
My hair blows in the summer breeze.
    My horse gallops on a winding road,
The road has so many curves,
    Like my life cycle throws.
Yet the ride helps me to clear my thoughts,
    Now I bring my horse to a trot,
She trots with such precision,
    Riding my horse was the right decision.
A ride of therapy, exactly what I envisioned!

WHOOO ARE YOU

Who is staring at me?
    With big yellow eyes and a rounded head,
It doesn't move, is he dead?
    I move closer…to get a look!
He has a beak with a hook.
    Only his eyes move…following me,
He just sits and waits patiently.
    He's like the lone ranger,
He wears a mask,
    Fears no danger, but I must ask,
Who are you? Whooo, Whooo

WINTER IS COMING

Off the road hopping along,
    Goes a frog singing his song.
Up the tree performing like a flying trapeze,
    Goes the squirrel with a nut surely to please.
Down the river the fishes go,
    Swift and smooth as they flow.
High in the sky free as can be,
    The birds are in flight heading southwardly.
The crickets in the night are playing their favorite melody,
    And the Locusts are hiding faithfully.
Now the groundhogs are gone and we surely know,
    We will soon see our very first snow.

YEAR OF THE TREE

If we keep chopping all our trees down,
There won't be any left standing around.
And all the animals who make them their home,
Will not have any place to call their own.
This could be a problem to society,
So every place you see empty,
Would you please….
Plant a tree!

A CRIPPLE'S CRY

While I'm sitting here at my window seat,
    I'm watching the butterflies go by.
Over yonder by a tree,
    Is a squirrel with a wandering eye.
There's children at play across the street,
    And the neighbors are mowing their lawn.
There is nothing I can do,
    For I am someone with something wrong.
I long for the days in my memory,
    When I could walk, play, and tease.
But now I'm in this punishment chair,
    For I'm a cripple and no one cares.
Oh how I long for the company,
    Of all my childhood friends.
When we use to talk so joyfully
    And the stories would never end.
I can hear the telephone ring,
    My mother rushes to answer.
I know it's not for me, as I said before
    No one wants a cripple knocking on their door.

So with these thoughts I sit and weep,
    And pray to God I'll see another week.
And for you out there who wonder why,
    Just look and listen for a cripple's cry.

Made in the USA
San Bernardino, CA
13 September 2015